1866-1991

125th

ANNIVERSARY

*Here's a list of some other
Redfeather Books from Henry Holt*

Great Whales: The Gentle Giants
by Patricia Lauber

*Something Special
by Emily Rodda

*Stargone John
by Ellen Kindt McKenzie

213 Valentines
by Barbara Cohen

*Weird Wolf
by Margery Cuyler

*Available in paperback

❖ ROBERT M. McCLUNG

Snakes ❖ ❖ ❖

Their Place in the Sun

illustrated by

DAVID M. DENNIS

A Redfeather Book

HENRY HOLT AND COMPANY ❖ NEW YORK

*Grateful acknowledgment is made to Carol Townsend,
Associate, Herpetology Department, American Museum of
Natural History, New York, for her careful reading of the
manuscript and her helpful suggestions.*

First published in 1979 by Garrard Publishing Company
Revised and expanded edition published in 1991 by
Henry Holt and Company
Published by Henry Holt and Company, Inc.,
115 West 18th Street, New York, New York 10011.
Published simultaneously in Canada by Fitzhenry & Whiteside Ltd.,
195 Allstate Parkway, Markham, Ontario L3R 4T8.

Library of Congress Cataloging-in-Publication Data
McClung, Robert M.
Snakes, their place in the sun / by Robert M. McClung;
illustrated by David M. Dennis.
(A Redfeather book)
Includes index.
Summary: Details the life cycle of snakes of the
eastern United States, including their place in the food chain
and their ecological value.
ISBN 0-8050-1718-6
1. Snakes—Juvenile literature. 2. Snakes—Pennsylvania—
Juvenile literature. [1. Snakes.] I. Dennis, David M.,
ill. II. Title. III. Series: Redfeather books.
QL666.06M2 1991
597.96—dc20 91-16312

Printed in the United States of America
on acid-free paper.∞

10 9 8 7 6 5 4 3 2 1

Permission for the use of the following photographs is gratefully acknowledged: page 9 (eastern
garter snake) © Runk / Schoenberger / Grant Heilman Photography, Inc.; page 19 (northern copperhead at den site) and page 29 (smooth green snakes hatching) © Zig Leszczynski; page 37
(western smooth green snake shedding its skin) © John C. Murphy / Tom Stack and Associates;
page 49 (red-shouldered hawk with garter snake) Animals / Animals © Joe McDonald.

❖ Contents

Snakes

Their Place in the Sun

1 ❖ *A Snake Goes Hunting*

A snake lies on a low stone wall beside the barn, sunning itself. The May night had been chilly, and the snake, a black racer, was cold when it came out of its den under the wall. It moved slowly. Lying on the rock, its body begins to soak up the heat of the spring sun.

Slender and sleek, the black racer is slightly more than three feet long. Its body is little more than an inch wide. Row after row of small scales cover the upper part of the snake's body. They overlap one another like shingles on a roof. The scales are smooth and shiny.

A single row of broad, crosswise scales covers the snake's belly. These broad scales are called scutes. The snake travels on them.

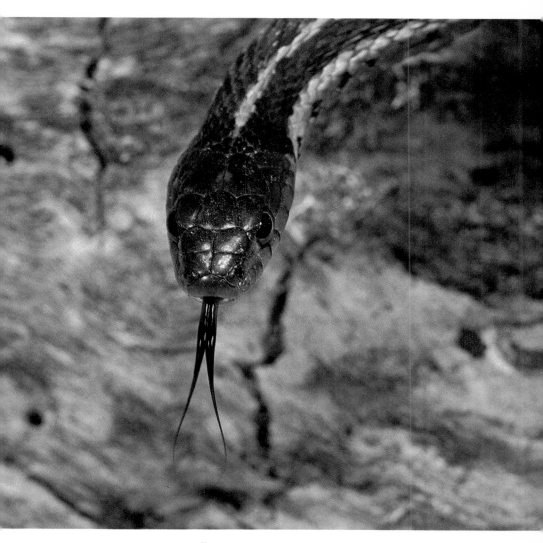

Eastern garter snake

Warmed by the sun, the black racer heads out into the meadow to hunt for food. Moving slowly, the snake flows through the grass like a glistening stream of water. Then, as it picks up speed, the racer moves ahead in smooth S-curves. Its scutes press against every stone and rough spot on the ground, helping to push its body forward. It is traveling at about three miles an hour.

Silently, the racer glides through the thick grass, searching for possible prey—a mouse, a baby bird, a frog, even another snake. The racer uses its eyes as it hunts, for snakes have very good eyesight at short distances.

Every few seconds, the racer's forked tongue flicks in and out. Like all snakes, it uses its tongue for picking up scents. The two tips of the tongue pick up tiny specks of matter from the ground and air. They carry the specks to two small pits in the snake's mouth. There the specks are tasted and smelled.

The black racer enters a narrow crack in a pile

A Snake's Body

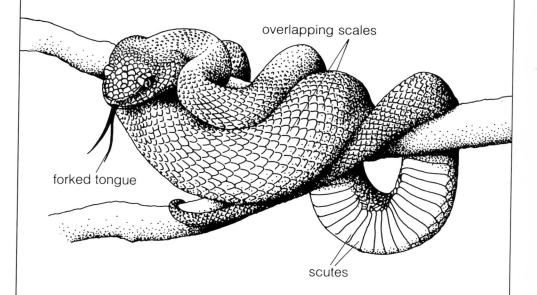

overlapping scales

forked tongue

scutes

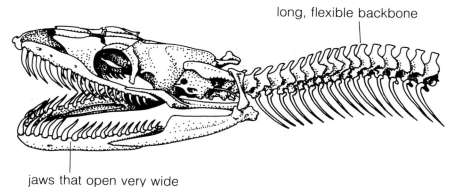

long, flexible backbone

jaws that open very wide

of rocks. It explores the space inside but finds no food.

Moving on, it comes to an old stump. At one side is a small hole leading to a burrow. The black racer's flicking tongue picks up the scent of a chipmunk. Entering the dark tunnel, the snake crawls to an underground nest. The chipmunk, however, is not at home. Turning, the snake crawls out again.

Nearby, a fat woodchuck is munching on clover. A robin flies overhead, carrying a squirming caterpillar in its beak. A sparrow hawk dives toward the ground and seizes a big, yellow butterfly. Other animals are getting food, but the snake has not yet found its meal.

The black racer travels on until it comes to the edge of the farm pond. Spotting a green frog on the bank, the racer lunges at it. The frog leaps away and escapes into the water. The snake crawls into the tall reeds and bushes at the upper end of the pond. Then it heads back toward the meadow.

The Senses of a Hunter

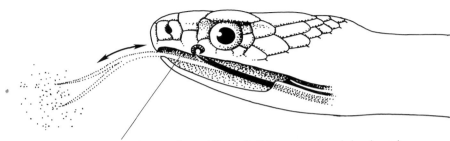

The Jacobson's organ "tastes" and "smells" the scents picked up by the tongue.

nostril

pit

Rattlesnakes are pit vipers. In addition to the senses that all snakes have, they can sense the body heat of their prey using these heat-sensitive pits.

How Snakes Move

Although snakes have no legs, they can move surprisingly quickly. Most snakes use a combination of the following basic movements to get around:

The *serpentine movement* is the most common way a snake moves. In this type of movement, the snake moves ahead in a series of S-curves. It presses its body against rocks, roots, or sticks to help push itself forward.

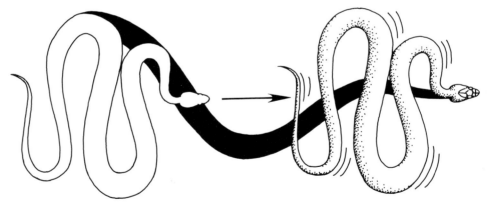

Some snakes travel through the branches of trees or on the ground in a *concertina movement*. Here, the snake moves its head and the front part of its body forward until they are straight, then pulls up the rest of its body in a series of loops.

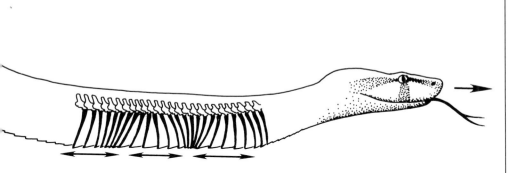

Big, heavy snakes like the anaconda often crawl ahead in straight lines known as the *caterpillar crawl*. As the snake glides along the ground, its belly scutes move ahead in successive, rippling waves.

Sidewinding is ideal for soft, sandy ground. That is why this sidewinder rattlesnake uses this movement to get around the desert. Pressing its tail and the back of its body into the sand, the snake throws a wide loop of its body out to one side, then draws the rear section up before throwing out another loop.

Ahead of the black racer, a red-tailed hawk dives at a cottontail rabbit. The rabbit thumps its feet in alarm as it whisks into a patch of briars to escape. The racer can hear those thumps even though it does not have ear openings, as we do. The bones in its lower jaw pick up the sound waves traveling through the ground. Other bones carry them to the snake's inner ears.

Soon the racer's flicking tongue picks up the fresh scent of a meadow mouse. Following the scent, the silent hunter finally sights its prey ahead. The plump little mouse is nibbling at a head of ripening seeds. It does not see the snake.

When the racer is within striking distance, it darts forward and seizes the mouse with its needle-sharp teeth. The mouse squeals in terror as a heavy loop of the snake's body pins it to the ground. When the mouse stops struggling, the racer shifts its grip and takes the head of the mouse in its jaws. The snake begins to swallow its meal.

A few minutes later, the farmer walks past.

When he sees the black racer with the partly swallowed mouse in its jaws, he smiles. Unlike many people, this farmer likes snakes. He knows that they eat many rats, mice, and other pests that damage his crops. The farmer is glad to have snakes make their homes on his farm.

2 ❖ *Where Snakes Live*

*M*ore than 2,400 different kinds of snakes live in the world today. Most of them are found in places where the weather is warm. But snakes live in almost all parts of the world. One, the Old World adder, ranges almost as far north as the Arctic Circle.

Nearly a dozen different kinds of snakes make their homes on the Pennsylvania farm where the black racer searches for its prey. Each kind has its own living place.

Some, like the black racer, live in the open meadows or in the fields of hay and grain. A number of garter snakes live in the orchards or in the big vegetable garden. Water snakes live in the farm pond and ribbon snakes roam the shores of

Northern copperhead at den site

the pond. Still other kinds of snakes live in the woodlot, the rocky hillside pasture, and the pine forest. Each of these places is a hunting ground for the snakes that inhabit it.

The territory in which each snake lives is called its home area or range. The snake seldom leaves that area. However, some snakes must travel to special places where they will spend the winter.

Somewhere within its home area, each snake has a shelter. This retreat is often called its den.

A snake does not dig a burrow for a home, as woodchucks do. It does not build a nest, as birds and mice do. A snake's shelter may be a hollow log or a natural cave under a stump or rock. It may be a space in a pile of stones or a crack in a stone wall. Often it is a burrow that used to belong to a fox, a chipmunk, or some other animal.

The snake sleeps in its den and hides there when danger threatens. It may go into the den to get away from the hot summer sun or to keep from getting chilled during cool fall nights.

Snakes and Their Relatives

Snakes are reptiles. Reptiles are a group of cold-blooded animals that have backbones and dry, scaly skins. There are five main groups of living reptiles. Here they are:

Lizards are the closest relatives of snakes.

Turtles and Tortoises have bodies that are covered by a hard shell.

Tuataras are the only survivors of a group of prehistoric reptiles.

There are more than 2,400 different species of *snakes* throughout the world.

Crocodilians are the largest of the reptiles.

Snakes on a Farm in Pennsylvania

There are many areas on the farm that provide living places for snakes. Different snakes live and hunt in different areas.

This black racer searches for small rodents and ground-nesting birds in the fields and meadows. It is sometimes found in bushes and the low branches of trees.

The pilot black snake roams the open pine woods. It can climb trees and sometimes takes young birds from their nests. It is also found in barns and old buildings where it feeds on rats and mice.

This ribbon snake searches for insects in the reeds along the shore of the pond.

Snakes and other reptiles, such as lizards and alligators, are all cold-blooded creatures. Their body heat comes from the sun, as they absorb warmth from the air, earth, or water around them. As a result, they must regulate their body temperatures by adjusting their activities to their surroundings. After a cool night, or when the air is chilly, a snake raises its body heat by basking in the warm rays of the sun. If the surroundings become too hot, it retreats into the shade or a cool burrow.

Mammals and birds, on the other hand, are what we call warm-blooded. They have special heat-regulating systems within their bodies. This allows them to maintain a fairly constant temperature inside their bodies, regardless of how warm or cold their immediate surroundings may be. Many warm-blooded animals have cooling systems such as sweat glands that get rid of heat that is not needed.

Reptiles do not have such heat-regulating systems. Yet, like birds and mammals, they must keep their body temperature fairly level. If a snake is kept under the blazing sun for too long, or at a temperature of 105 degrees Fahrenheit or more, it soon dies.

If the outside temperature goes below 50 degrees Fahrenheit, the snake becomes cold and sluggish. It needs a higher temperature in order to remain active. If the temperature approaches freezing, the snake must find shelter, or it will die just as surely as if it gets too hot.

How does a snake keep its body temperature within the right limits?

One way is simply by moving. If its surroundings become too hot, the snake crawls into a cooler spot. In very warm, sunny weather it may stay in its burrow all day long and come out only at night.

When autumn comes, that same snake may become most active during daylight hours, when the sun warms the air. During much cooler nights, it usually stays in its burrow.

In many regions, winter brings snow and

freezing temperatures. Here, snakes must find some safe shelter as cold weather approaches. Then they can sink into a deep winter sleep known as hibernation. If they cannot find such a sheltered spot, they will freeze to death.

Once fall comes in such regions, snakes begin to travel toward the places where they will hibernate. These may be cracks in a rock ledge that lead to sheltered spaces deep underground. They may be deep caves, or snug burrows beneath logs or rocks. Snakes of several different kinds sometimes gather by the hundreds in such shelters. Some return to the same place year after year. Long before winter arrives, the snakes crawl underground. The temperature in their dens always remains above freezing, no matter how cold it is outside.

Safely sheltered, the snakes soon become motionless. They seem to be lifeless, but they are not. They remain in this state all winter long.

Spring finally approaches. The days become longer and the air warmer. The earth warms up too. As the temperature rises, the hibernating snakes sense the change. Little by little, they become active. One warm day, some of them crawl into the bright sunshine. Soon all of them take up their warm-weather lives once again.

3 ❖ How Snakes Are Born

Spring is courtship time for snakes on the farm. One warm morning in May, a male black racer comes upon the trail of a female black racer. The odor from her skin and from glands near the base of her tail signals that she is ready for mating. Tongue flicking, the male black racer follows the trail. After several hours, he finds the female. He rushes at her several times, then crawls up beside her and rubs his chin across her back. His body coils about her and soon they are mating.

In midsummer, a few weeks after mating, the female black racer searches out a fallen log at the edge of the woods. The ground beneath it is soft and crumbly, full of rotting leaves and wood. Burrowing into this mass, the black racer lays her eggs—about two dozen of them.

Smooth green snakes hatching

The eggs of the black racer had been developing within her body for some months before she mated. Each egg contained a large amount of yolk, food for the developing snake. After the female mated, her eggs were fertilized and the baby snakes began to develop within the eggs. Then the female laid her eggs and left them to develop on their own.

Under the fallen log, the black racer eggs are hidden from many enemies that might find and eat them. A hungry skunk or opossum would gobble them down if it found them. So would a crow or jay.

If they get too much moisture, the eggs may become moldy. The snakes growing inside the eggs may die if the eggs become too wet, too dry, too hot, or too cold. The temperature and humidity also affect the rate of development of the young. Under the log, the eggs are likely to get the moisture and warmth they need.

It is easy to tell that these are not bird eggs.

Snake Babies Come from Eggs

The black racer, like most egg-laying snakes, leaves her eggs to hatch
on their own.

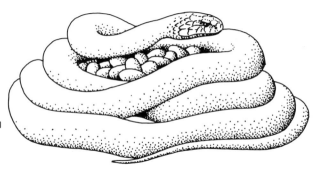

The female king cobra
is one of the few
snakes that stays with
her eggs until they are
ready to hatch. She
coils up on top of them
to protect them.

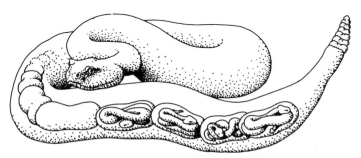

Rattlesnake eggs stay inside the mother's body until the baby snakes
are ready to be born.

A bird's egg usually has one big end and one small end. But like all snake eggs, the black racer's are long and curved alike at both ends. The white shell is thick and leathery.

When it is ready to hatch, the baby snake inside uses a tiny egg tooth at the tip of its snout. It cuts a slit in the shell and sticks its head out. After resting a bit, it crawls completely out of the crumpled shell.

On the same spring morning that the black racers mate, a male timber rattlesnake follows the scent trail of a female rattlesnake, high up on the hillside. Both of them are still close to the rocky ledge where they slept through the winter.

After a few minutes, the male rattler meets another male following the same trail. The two rear up and face each other, tongues flicking. They twine their bodies together and sway back and forth.

Each male attempts to push the other off balance. Each seems to be trying to show that he is

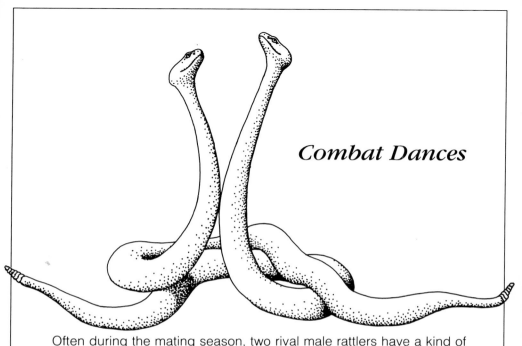

Combat Dances

Often during the mating season, two rival male rattlers have a kind of contest called a combat dance. Such behavior, like courtship battles between male deer and many other male animals, may ensure that the larger and stronger male will go on to mate with the female.

the stronger. The two males do not hurt each other, however. Finally, one male gives up and crawls away. The other goes on to find the female and mate with her.

Although the black racer, and many other snakes on the farm, lay eggs and leave them to

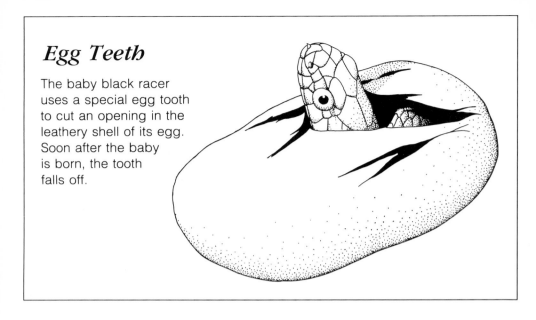

Egg Teeth

The baby black racer uses a special egg tooth to cut an opening in the leathery shell of its egg. Soon after the baby is born, the tooth falls off.

hatch, the rattlesnake does not. Rattlesnake eggs stay in the female's body until the young are ready to be born. A female rattlesnake may give birth to as many as twenty babies.

Each baby rattlesnake usually comes out of the mother's body wrapped in a thin, soft covering. The young break free of this wrapping almost at once. Each baby rattler has fangs and poison on the day of its birth. It is ready to hunt for whatever small prey it can get.

Like the mother rattlesnake, several other kinds of female snakes on the farm, including the water snake, the copperhead, and the garter snake, bear living young. However, most female snakes throughout the world lay their eggs. On the farm, baby hognose snakes, pilot black snakes, and milk snakes are just a few of the snakes that hatch from eggs.

By late summer, there are lots of young snakes on the farm. A number of the baby snakes are no bigger than earthworms. They hunt small insects for their food. They swallow tiny toads and frogs.

Many of these young snakes will be eaten, or will die in some other way, before they have a chance to grow up. Hawks, crows, and other birds gobble down many of them. Skunks and other mammals eat still more. But some of the little snakes will survive. It is nature's way to make sure that enough young are born so that some will live to become adults and have young of their own.

4 ❖ *Eating and Growing*

One of the baby snakes that survived that fall is a milk snake. It hatched in August from a clutch of ten eggs laid under a pile of logs near the farmer's barn. It was just nine inches long. Because milk snakes often live near barns, some people think they suck milk from cows. That is how these snakes got their name. But this old folktale is entirely false. Milk snakes eat rats, mice, and other small animals.

During the fall, the young milk snake eats many insects, tiny earthworms, and other small creatures. It sheds its skin and adds nearly two inches to its length before cold weather arrives. That winter, it hibernates in a deep burrow under the pile of logs. During the spring and summer, it

Western smooth green snake shedding its skin

eats many baby mice and other small animals. That fall, when it is a year old, it measures nearly seventeen inches in length. It is almost twice as long as it had been when it hatched.

A year later, it has grown another four inches. Most of its growth took place in the spring and summer. Snakes grow fastest during warm weather, when they are actively hunting and eating.

One June morning in the summer of its third year, the milk snake lies coiled in its den under the pile of logs. The den is near the cornfield and the hayfield, and close to the farm buildings as well. The milk snake has found it a good place to live. There is always good hunting nearby.

The milk snake on the farm is not hungry this morning. A few days earlier, its scales had become rough and dull, and a cloudy whiteness had appeared in its eyes. The time has come for the snake to shed its skin. As they grow, snakes usually shed their skin several times each year.

Crawling out of its den, the snake glides

through the brush, rubbing its head against rough stones and bark. First, the old skin loosens around the snake's lips. Then it begins to peel back. It looks like crumpled tissue paper. As the snake crawls over other rough surfaces, the skin peels back farther over its body.

Finally, the skin is peeled all the way off. It is inside out and all in one piece. The milk snake's new skin is clean, bright, and shiny.

The snake is soon hungry again. It goes hunting, and near the corncrib it comes upon a young rat gnawing at an ear of corn. Crawling closer, the milk snake suddenly lunges forward with open jaws. The snake's sharp teeth seize the rat. Its scaly body pins the rat to the ground. Then the snake quickly wraps several coils of its body around the struggling victim. The coils tighten. Soon the rat cannot breathe. In a few moments it is dead.

Loosening its grip, the snake takes the rat's nose in its jaws. It is getting ready to swallow its meal. A snake's teeth do not tear or chew. They

Open Wide

Your jaws move so that your mouth can open wide, but a snake's jaws are made to allow its mouth to open much wider. That's a good thing, because snakes never chew their food. They swallow it whole.

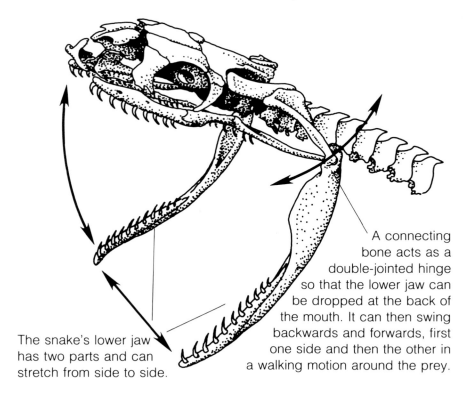

A connecting bone acts as a double-jointed hinge so that the lower jaw can be dropped at the back of the mouth. It can then swing backwards and forwards, first one side and then the other in a walking motion around the prey.

The snake's lower jaw has two parts and can stretch from side to side.

simply hold the prey, which is always swallowed whole. But the rat is much bigger around than the snake is. How can the snake swallow it?

The secret is that a snake's jaw can stretch. The upper jaw has two separate parts—one on the right side and one on the left. So does the lower jaw. Each part can move by itself. It can stretch away from all the other parts. It can shift away from the other bones of the skull. Because of this, a snake can stretch its whole head to swallow a meal.

The milk snake is holding the rat firmly with the jaws and teeth on the right side of its head. It moves the jaws on the left side forward to get a new grip. Then it moves the right jaws forward. Left jaw, right jaw, left jaw, right jaw: the rat goes down the snake's throat very slowly, a bit at a time. Finally, it disappears.

All snakes swallow their prey in this way. Some, like the garter snake and black racer, begin to swallow their victims as soon as they seize them.

Others, like the milk snake, squeeze their prey until it dies. Such snakes are called constrictors, for they squeeze, or constrict, their prey.

Other snakes besides the milk snake are out searching for food this morning, too. The farm is home to many kinds of snakes. There is plenty of food for all, because snakes hunt in different ways, and at different times of the day.

Snakes seek prey of different sizes. Big snakes hunt big animals, while little snakes take much smaller prey. So two snakes hunting in the same place may be looking for different kinds of food.

In the orchard that morning, a garter snake catches a little toad and eats it. Another garter snake swallows an earthworm.

In the pasture, a hognose snake seizes a half-grown cowbird from a nest on the ground. A black racer finds a nest of mice just a few days old. It eats every one of them.

A brightly striped ribbon snake searches for little frogs and toads along the edge of the farm

Time for Lunch?

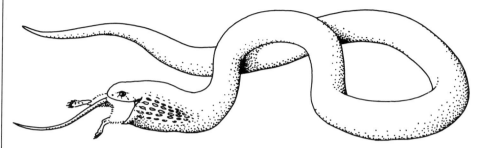

The larger the prey, the less often a snake has to eat. Many snakes eat only once or twice a week.

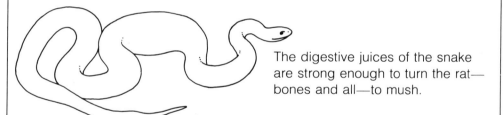

The digestive juices of the snake are strong enough to turn the rat—bones and all—to mush.

After the digestive juices have done their work, the soft waste material is cast out. Now the snake is ready to begin hunting for its next meal.

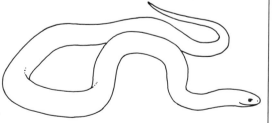

pond. A big water snake seizes a catfish, and a smaller one swallows a bullfrog tadpole. At the edge of the woodlot, a green snake climbs into a bush, where it feeds on caterpillars.

A big, black rat snake, or pilot black snake, lives near the pine woods on the hillside. It is an expert climber. Approaching an old pine tree, it begins to crawl up the trunk.

Twenty feet above the ground, the big snake crawls out on a limb. It is heading for a nest with three young blue jays. Just then, the mother jay returns with a meal of insects for her hungry young.

Dropping the food, the mother jay screams in alarm and dives to attack the snake. Her mate quickly joins her. They peck at the snake so fiercely that it gives up. It comes down from the tree and goes off to hunt for an easier meal.

That evening, a timber rattlesnake crawls out of its den farther up the slope. It usually hunts at night, for it does not need to see its prey to locate it. The moon has not yet appeared, and the night is very dark. Flicking out its tongue, the snake picks up the scent of a cottontail rabbit. The prey is hidden in the darkness somewhere ahead. The snake cannot see the rabbit, but it can find it just the same.

A rattlesnake has two hollows, or pits, on its face. These help it to find prey. Each pit is lined with nerve endings that record tiny changes in air temperature. They sense the body heat of a nearby warm-blooded animal. They tell the snake that its prey is close at hand.

The trail becomes fresher as the timber rattler closes in on its prey. Finally, its pits record the body heat of an animal just ahead.

Now the rattlesnake is about to use its special weapons, its fangs. These are two long, curved teeth in the upper jaws. When they are not in use, they are folded back like the blades of a jackknife. When the snake opens its mouth to strike, the fangs spring upright. They are ready for action.

The fangs are hollow. Each is connected to a sac of poison in the upper jaw. When the rattle-

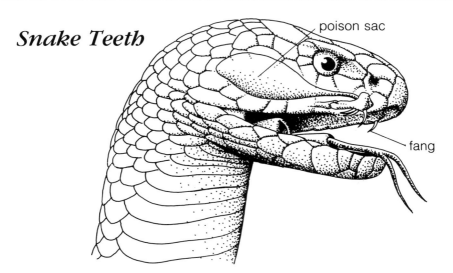

Snake Teeth

poison sac

fang

A cobra's needle-sharp teeth are for grabbing, not chewing. It has several special, hollow teeth called fangs.

snake strikes, muscles squeeze the sacs. They force poison through the fangs and into the prey.

Closing in on the rabbit, the rattlesnake rears up. Its body lunges forward as it strikes at the prey. It sinks its long, curved fangs deep into the rabbit's side, then quickly withdraws them.

The rabbit jumps in surprise and staggers a few feet forward. It falls over and kicks its hind legs several times. Then it dies. The rattler's poison works very quickly. Approaching its prey, the snake begins to swallow it.

Many snakes on the farm capture meals that day and night. But some snakes are eaten by other animals on the farm.

A big rat finds a baby milk snake near the barn and kills and eats it. Just the week before, however, an adult milk snake had eaten a whole litter of baby rats.

A skunk finds some of the black racer's eggs along the edge of the woods and eats them. On the hillside, a big raccoon kills a year-old pilot black snake and eats it. The raccoon does not know it, but the father of that little pilot black snake had eaten one of the raccoon's babies several months before.

Snakes hunt many kinds of animals for food. Many of those same animals also hunt snakes and eat them. Thus, each group helps to control the population of the other. All of these hunters help to keep nature's balance.

5 ❖ How Nature Keeps a Balance

*M*any kinds of plants grow on the farm. The farm is a small one, owned by the same family for three generations. Unlike owners of big farms who usually specialize in one crop, this Pennsylvania farmer plants a number of different crops—hay, corn, wheat, oats, and potatoes—and keeps a small herd of dairy cattle as well. The farmer feeds some of the grain that he grows to his horses, cows, and pigs. His family also eats some of it.

The farmer plants a big vegetable garden every year, and in the fall he picks fruit in his orchard. His hayfields supply winter fodder for his cows and other livestock, and the pastures furnish food for them during other seasons. Acorns and other nuts grow in the woodlot, and many kinds

Red-shouldered hawk with garter snake

of berries grow along the fences. Some of these plants provide food for the farmer and his live-stock. Nearly all are food for plant-eating wild animals on the farm.

Grasses, clover, and many other plants grow in open fields. Seed-eating mice and birds live there. They can find plenty of the food they need in the fields. Nearly every day, from spring until late fall, some of the mice and baby birds are eaten by snakes. Once in a while, a hawk or a crow swoops down on a snake and makes a meal of it.

Seed to meadow mouse to snake to hawk— each is one link in what scientists call a food chain. All of the plants and animals in any one area are linked in many such food chains.

Green plants are the first links, for they make their own food, using energy from the sun. The food is then stored in stalks, seeds, fruits, and other parts of the plant.The next links are the plant-eating animals—the countless insects, mammals, birds, and other animals that feed on plants.

The Food Chain

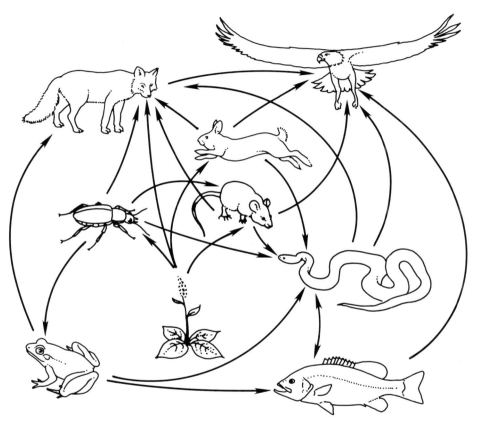

Every living thing needs food in order to live, to give it energy, and to help it grow. Every animal eats something else in order to stay alive. In the typical food chain, tiny animals are eaten by meat-eating animals, and the big meat-eaters hunt smaller animals, both plant-eaters and meat-eaters. Snakes are always meat-eaters, and play an important role in the balance of nature.

All over the farm, insects eat leaves or other parts of plants. Butterflies float from blossom to blossom in the meadow, sipping nectar. Bees gather loads of nectar and pollen in the orchard.

In the pasture, a goldfinch eats thistle seeds. At the edge of the woodlot, a chipmunk nibbles on berries. A fat woodchuck and many cottontails fill up on clover in the hayfield.

A flock of starlings gobbles down grain in the fields of wheat and corn. And so, of course, do the mice.

After the plant-eating animals, the next links in the food chain are the meat-eaters.

Spiders sit in their webs, waiting for flying insects. Shiny dragonflies swoop across the farm pond, catching mosquitoes and flies. Warblers and many other birds fill up on caterpillars. Moles and shrews travel through underground tunnels, searching for earthworms and beetle grubs.

Snakes also eat the earthworms and grubs, as well as mice, birds, and all sorts of other creatures.

One evening, a fox catches a rabbit at the edge of the woods, and a screech owl pounces on a white-footed mouse. A raccoon eats a frog on the edge of the pond, and a skunk digs up the eggs of a snapping turtle and eats them. In the water, a tiny sunfish eats a mosquito wriggler. Then a little water snake catches the sunfish. But before the snake can eat the fish, a big snapping turtle seizes the snake and eats it.

From plants to plant-eating animals to meat-eaters—the energy that comes from eating is passed along in the food chain.

The snakes that live on the farm are important links in many food chains.

A baby garter snake crawls across a field, and a crow flying overhead spots it. Swooping down, the crow kills the little snake and swallows it.

In the pine woods, a big pilot black snake seizes a half-grown red squirrel. Wrapping its coils about the struggling rodent, the black snake squeezes it to death before eating it.

Some snakes hunt other snakes for food. The king cobra of Southeast Asia dines almost exclusively on other snakes. The American king snake includes snakes in its diet.

A number of other reptiles are snake-eaters too. Crocodiles and alligators snap up those they catch in the water. Some big lizards eat small snakes whenever they have the opportunity.

Many birds hunt snakes. Chief among them are the birds of prey—eagles, hawks, and owls. The swift roadrunner of our southwestern states also pursues and devours many small snakes.

Skunks, weasels, raccoons, and foxes are just a few of the mammals that sometimes eat snakes. Pigs eat them too. They do not seem to be affected by the venom of poisonous snakes.

Snakes have many enemies. They also have many ways of protecting themselves. Some, like the copperhead and the green snake, have colors and patterns that blend into their surroundings.

Camouflage

Some snakes manage to blend into their environment so well that they are almost invisible to other animals. This does two things. It helps the snakes to hide from their enemies, and it means that the snakes can hide, unseen by its prey, until it is ready to strike.

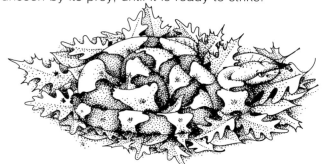

This copperhead is almost invisible among the autumn leaves.

Hiding under the sun-dappled palmetto fronds, this diamondback rattlesnake can hardly be seen.

They are hard for an enemy to spot. Often they go unseen.

If it is seen, a snake usually tries to escape. It may crawl away or glide into a burrow or narrow space where the enemy cannot follow.

If it is cornered, the snake usually faces its enemy. Sometimes it tries to scare the other animal away by hissing in a threatening manner. The rattlesnake coils. Its buzzing rattles sound a warning. If its opponent comes on, the rattlesnake defends itself with its fangs and poison.

The hognose snake puffs up its body so that it looks much bigger than usual. If this does not scare off the enemy, the snake rolls over on its back and plays dead. It plays dead so well that the enemy usually leaves it alone.

Sometimes a curious enemy rolls the hognose snake right side up. Then, as if to show that it really is dead, the snake quickly rolls bottom side up once again.

The common garter snake defends itself in another way. If attacked or picked up, the garter snake gives off a bad-smelling liquid. The smell may make the other animal drop the snake and go away.

The poisonous coral snakes of the southern United States stay out of sight most of the time. When they do venture out, however, their bold patterns of bright red, yellow, and black advertise their presence and warn other animals not to come too close. If an animal does get bitten by a coral snake and survives the painful encounter, it learns to avoid all snakes with similar bright colors.

Several nonpoisonous snakes, among them the scarlet king snake, probably gain some protection because their patterns and vivid colors resemble those of the coral snakes. Sighting them, their enemies may leave these snakes alone because they mistake them for the poisonous species.

Snakes can defend themselves against other animals in a variety of ways. But they cannot defend themselves against the changes human beings make in nature. People are their greatest enemies.

People upset the lives of snakes and other animals nearly everywhere they live and work. Such human activities as land clearing, draining swamps, forestry, plowing, cultivating, and road building destroy or alter much of the living space that many plant and wildlife species need.

When land is covered with buildings and parking lots, snakes and other animals lose their living space. When water is polluted, animals often cannot drink it or live in it. When air is polluted, animals suffer. The poisons used to kill insect pests kill other animals as well.

Snakes are harmed by these changes. So are other animals. But snakes suffer still another kind of harm. Many people fear and hate snakes. They kill snakes every chance they get.

In many areas where rattlesnakes live, community groups stage snake-killing parties every spring in the areas where they are known to hibernate. They often kill them by the hundreds as the rattlers venture out from their winter dens.

Great numbers of snakes are killed on highways each year too. The wide ribbons of concrete absorb heat during the day. At night, when the air is cooler, the roads are still warm. Snakes crawl onto the roadways and lie there, soaking up the heat. As a result, passing cars kill many snakes.

Today, snakes are disappearing rapidly in countless areas where they were once common. Many kinds of snakes are becoming endangered because of human activities and prejudices. The timber rattlesnake is rapidly disappearing in New York, New Jersey, and many other parts of its range. The king snakes, the indigo snake, and various kinds of garter snakes, among others, are also disappearing because of human destruction of their natural environment.

Most people do not understand how important snakes are to all of us. They do not realize that snakes are a meat-eating link in many food chains. They do not realize that snakes play an important

Snakes in Danger

More and more snakes are becoming endangered species. Here are some of the many snakes that were once plentiful but are now in danger of disappearing.

The shy San Francisco garter snake has begun to disappear as large areas of marshland have been developed for housing or industry.

The Eastern indigo snake prefers to live in undisturbed natural areas. As these have been destroyed to make way for houses and farms, the snakes have become rare. It's a popular snake to keep as a pet, and so it has been over-collected.

The New Mexican ridgenose rattlesnake has always been rare and is becoming even more scarce as its habitat is destroyed. Its existence is also threatened by over-collection.

role in helping to keep nature's balance.

Plants and animals that live together form a community of living things. Each member affects its neighbors in various ways. All are somehow linked together.

We, too, are part of the community of living things. That is why the farmer smiles when he sees a snake eating a rat, mouse, or other pest that damages his crop. He knows that snakes are important in nature's balance. He knows that they have a right to their place in the sun.

❖ *Index*

Italic indicates picture.

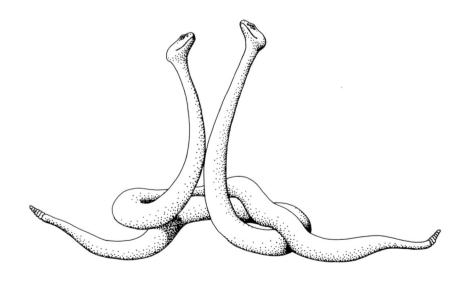